About this Book

The Curse of the Lost Idol is a mystery story with a difference. The difference is that you have to solve the mystery yourself.

Throughout the book, there are puzzles which you must solve for the next part of the story to make sense. Clues and evidence lurk in the words and the pictures.

Keep your wits about you as you read the story and look carefully at the pictures. Don't turn over to the next page until you have found the solution.

Some of the puzzles relate to previous pages so you may have to flick back through the book to find a vital piece of information.

If you get stuck, there are extra clues to help you on page 41. They are printed in a secret way, so you will have to work out how to read them first. If you are completely stuck and have to admit defeat, all the answers are on pages 42 to 48.

This is Annie. She manages to solve the mystery. Can you?

The Amazing Discovery

Professor Pott and his eager assistant, Eric, were excavating near an ancient Egyptian temple. After weeks of hot, sweaty digging they had only found boring bits of pot and a few old bones. One day, something extraordinary happened . . .

The Professor lurched forwards as the ground gave way beneath his spade.

They cleared away the loose sand to reveal a dark, gaping hole in the ground.

Eric threw a stone into the hole and waited . . . and waited to hear it fall.

Eric unravelled his handy, portable rope ladder and secured it to a large boulder. The Professor climbed gingerly down into the deep, dark hole.

Eric joined the Professor at the bottom. They were standing in an underground chamber. Eric shivered. He hoped it wasn't a tomb full of mummies.

CURSE
of the
LOST IDOL

Gaby Waters

Designed and illustrated by
Graham Round

Contents

The Professor shone his flashlight on the walls while Eric stumbled about in the gloom.

Suddenly he collided with a cold, hard object in the middle of the chamber.

Eric took the flashlight, expecting the worst. But he could not believe his eyes.

"A golden statue!" he squeaked in amazement. "With six toes!"

The Professor gasped and staggered. "Good grief... It's the lost idol!"

Even Eric knew of the lost idol. Long ago, it was said to possess mysterious, magical powers and it was worshipped throughout Ancient Egypt. 3000 years ago, the

High Priest hid the idol in a secret underground chamber to protect it. Since that time many people have searched for the idol, but always in vain ... until today.

An Ancient Curse

Eric gawped at the idol in stunned silence. He tried to lift it off the stone plinth, but his weedy biceps could not cope with the weight.

"Pure gold is very heavy," said the Professor, straining every muscle to hold the idol.

"Look! Hieroglyphics!" said Eric excitedly.

He pointed to the stone plinth on which the idol stood gleaming in the torchlight. They saw row upon row of strange pictures and intricate symbols exquisitely carved into the crumbling surface. Eric knew that centuries had passed since the last eyes had looked on the ancient message. He watched the Professor turn pale as he worked out the meaning of the mysterious symbols.

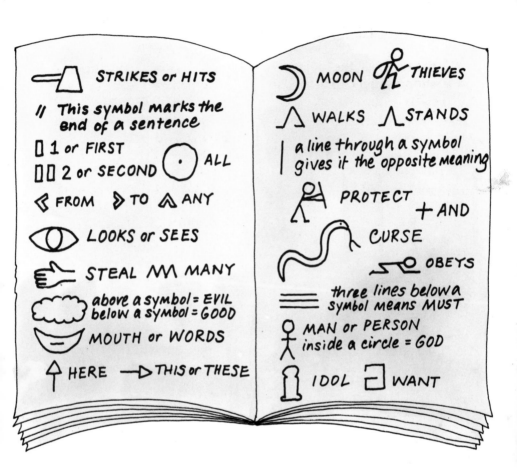

"It's a curse," said the Professor in a serious voice. "We must protect the idol. If we fail . . . who knows what might happen."

"But nothing can happen to the idol," Eric protested.

"I'm not so sure," replied the Professor. "What about the notorious Doppel Gang? They have masterminded numerous daring robberies and they go for ancient gold treasures every time. The idol is an obvious target."

"Wow!" said Eric, amazed that he could be caught up in anything so important and exciting.

"Exactly," said the Professor. "We shall have to be very careful. I must devise a plan . . . and you, Eric, must help me."

DON'T TURN THE PAGE YET

**Use the Professor's notebook to work out the meaning of the curse on the stone plinth.
What does it say?**

In the News

A few days later, the Professor's fabulous discovery hit the news headlines. It caused a sensation all over the world.

Annie was fascinated by the news of the discovery and longed to see the idol. Then she spotted the competition in The Daily Wheeze. It was tricky but she puzzled out the solution. Now, perhaps, there was a chance.

DON'T TURN THE PAGE YET

Solve the Riddle of the Sphinx.

The Daily
WHEEZE

GOSSIP
HEARSAY
RUMOUR
we print
it!

EUREKA!

POTT POTS MORE THAN A POT FOR POSTERITY

The inside story

By Sam Scoop in Cairo

Last Tuesday, deep beneath the windswept sands of the arid Egyptian desert, Professor Parsifal Pott made the discovery of a lifetime. Hardly daring to believe it, he unearthed the legendary "lost" idol – the greatest find since Tutankhamun's treasures were brought to light in 1922.

A unique treasure

The idol is no ordinary Egyptian statue. It is priceless – cast in purest gold with rare sapphires and emeralds inlaid around its head and a magnificent diamond in its back.

An ancient mystery

The idol is shrouded in mystery and magic. From its forehead rears the magic symbol of a one-eyed cobra and on its left foot there are six toes. It is also said to bear a powerful ancient curse.

Professor Pott: "I was stunned."

No idle threat

In an exclusive interview, the Professor delivered an awesome warning.

"Don't doubt the curse. It is as powerful today as it was in ancient times."

No exhibition

For these reasons, there are no plans for a public exhibition. The Professor is taking no chances. No photographs have been released and the location of the discovery site is top secret.

Potty Prof reveals all to lucky few

But! The Professor has generously offered to reveal the idol to a privileged few. Six lucky Wheeze readers will travel to Egypt to the secret site and see with their own eyes the fabulous lost idol. Solve the Riddle of the Sphinx and you stand a chance of winning this trip of a lifetime.

COMPETITION CORNER
THE RIDDLE OF THE SPHINX

The sphinx wanted to know which one of three gods stole the golden apple. Was it HORUS, ANUBIS or OSIRIS?

"I DIDN'T," said Horus.
"OSIRIS DID," said Anubis.

"ANUBIS IS LYING," said Osiris.

The sphinx knew that one god was telling the truth and the other two were lying.

WHICH ONE STOLE THE GOLDEN APPLE?

Send your answer to The Daily Wheeze, Cairo Office, Egypt.

9

Annie in Egypt

Several weeks later, Annie stood in the hot sunshine pinching herself. It hurt so much she knew she wasn't dreaming. She really was in Egypt.

She rummaged in her big bag. As usual, it was bulging with a strange collection of junk including a pocket mirror, magnetic toothpick, electric torch, extra sharp penknife and a bent tin whistle. At last she found what she was searching for: her prize-winner's letter. The instructions were perplexing.

"On arrival in Egypt, the steam boat with more than one funnel, at least 14 port side windows, a stern deck, a blue stripe but no flag will transport you up the River Nile to your secret destination. Please embark immediately."

Annie groaned as she looked at the boats moored along the quay. How many more puzzles would she have to solve? But on second thoughts, this puzzle was not so tricky. Annie raced towards the boat.

DON'T TURN THE PAGE YET

Which boat does Annie go to?

The Perplexing Plan

LOWER DECK (NOT DRAWN T

YOU ARE HERE

LARGE BALL ROOM

SMALL BALL ROOM

DELUXE CABIN

ANOTHER CABIN

SMALL BACK DECK

SPARE CABIN

TINY CABIN

1ST BATH ROOM

2ND BATH ROOM

LONG ROOM

EGYPTIAN BATH & SAUNA

STAIRS

STORE ROOM

STAIRS

PINK CABIN

PURPLE CABIN

BLUE CABIN

GREEN CABIN

YOU ARE HERE

Annie panted up the gangplank just as the mooring ropes were cast off. There was no one in sight and Annie wondered if she had made a mistake. Where were the other passengers?

Then she heard a stomping, swooshing sound coming up behind her. She spun round to find the source of the noise

looking up at her – a little person with an enormous moustache, wearing big boots and a baggy sort of nightshirt.

"Hello, my name's Annie," she said, trying hard not to stare at his outsize moustache. "What should I do next?"

"Join the others," he squeaked. "Go along the deck, take the first

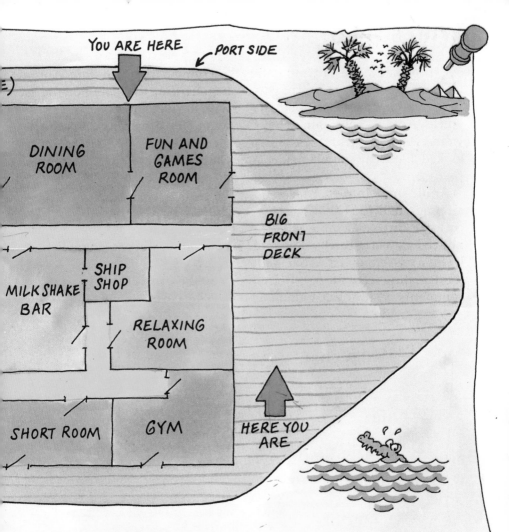

YOU ARE HERE

PORT SIDE

DINING ROOM

FUN AND GAMES ROOM

BIG FRONT DECK

MILK SHAKE BAR

SHIP SHOP

RELAXING ROOM

SHORT ROOM

GYM

HERE YOU ARE

corridor on the left, second passage on the right, turn right, turn left and left again, first right and it's the first door on the left." And then he scurried away.

Annie gulped, hoping she would remember the instructions. Then she spotted a boat plan, pinned to a lifebelt. It was hopeless. There were four arrows indicating YOU ARE HERE.

She stared hard at the plan for a moment or two. Then she smiled.

DON'T TURN THE PAGE YET

This is the boat plan.
  Where is Annie?
  Which room should she go to and what is her route?

Who's Who?

Annie knew she had found the right room. It was full of people talking at the tops of their voices. Annie's heart sank. They were a very odd lot and one or two looked distinctly suspicious.

Annie slunk into a corner sipping a delicious Nile Nectar cocktail. On a small table, she noticed a sheet of thick notepaper. It was a passenger list. What made it interesting were the cryptic comments beside each name.

Trying hard not to stare, Annie began fitting the names on the list with the faces in the room. It wasn't too difficult, but one thing puzzled her . . . apart from the waiters, there was one name missing.

DON'T TURN THE PAGE YET

You can see the passenger list below.
Fit the names to the faces.
Whose name is missing?

Passenger list

Annie — inquisitive and good at puzzle solving

Devilla de Visp — very fond of gold jewellery

Dr Boffin — expert on Egyptian idols

Terry Trubble — ex bank robber with a stutter

Luigi Macaroni — suspicious character with an Italian accent

Drusilla P. Culia — ancient curses fanatic – wears strange flowery clothes

Professor Pott — brilliant archaeologist

Sam Scoop — Daily Wheeze reporter - does anything for a good newspaper story

Harriet Flash — Daily Wheeze photographer – good friend of Sam Scoop

15

The Mysterious Message

That night, Annie lay awake in her narrow cabin bunk, listening to the water lapping against the sides of the boat. Every so often she thought she heard a chomping noise. Crocodiles? Impossible. There weren't any crocodiles in the river – were there?

But she could definitely hear something. This time there was a clumping sound as well. It was the sort of noise made by someone wearing boots that are far too big.

Annie decided to investigate. She crept to the door in bare feet and took a deep breath ready to face whatever monster lurked outside. Then she pushed against the door with all her might.

The door flew open with a loud crash. Annie heard a high pitched squeal as she lunged into the little person with a lopsided moustache. He was chewing a very sticky toffee.

"I'm very sorry, Mr . . ." Annie said, feeling very embarrassed.

The little person said nothing. He rearranged his moustache and pointed at an envelope lying on the deck.

Annie was puzzled. She opened the envelope cautiously and examined the contents. It contained a hand-drawn map and a crumpled scrap of paper. Annie read its mysterious message – it wasn't easy. She didn't really believe the message. It seemed too silly for words.

DON'T TURN THE PAGE YET

What does the message say?

tHee idle is in GRAAtE
                          daanjer. a
Bunch of roFLEss krooks Aree After
it aND i aM wurrid. rimember the
thE kerss OF tHe idle...... iT wIll

tAKe ittz rivENj. kip yoR eyes oppen
and be wair. trust noone. GUD LUK

P.S. here is a map. it mite bee usful — you
          nerver no.

Inside the Buried Chamber

The next day, Annie and all the other passengers (except for the nameless one) set off for the buried chamber.

Professor Pott led them off the boat along a dusty path into the desert. It was baking hot and Annie longed to stop at one of the refreshment stands beside the road. In the distance she saw some rocky hills and wondered how much further it was. She panted on, passing ruins on her left and an oasis on her right. Further on, they took a left turn and came to a building surrounded by fallen masonry. This was the Temple of the Moon God. Just beyond it was the entrance to the buried chamber.

Annie made the perilous descent down the rope ladder into the buried chamber. She gazed at the smooth, flat, walls covered in paintings. She was surprised by the soft sandy floor.

Then she saw the idol – gleaming in the gloomy light. The Professor told everyone to stand back. Dr Boffin pulled out his magnifying glass and was about to examine the idol when . . .

Don't panic ... it's just a temporary electrical failure.

... all of a sudden, the chamber was plunged into total darkness. Disembodied screams of shock rang out through the blackness. Annie could see nothing so she listened instead. She heard the Professor's voice and in the background there was a strange, scraping, digging sound.

Suddenly, without warning, the light came back. All at once, Annie knew something was wrong ... very wrong. The idol was missing!

Remember the curse. It will take its revenge.

With a sickening jolt, Annie remembered the mystery message. Too late. Drusilla broke the awful silence with a wail and panic broke out as everyone rushed for the ladder. Annie thought fast. Was there anything she could do? There was only one thing. Hastily, she took a few snaps with her Instantpic camera. Maybe they would contain clues that would lead to the thief.

Sandstorm!

At the top of the shaft everything was dark – not pitch black, but thick and murky. A vicious wind was blowing and Annie's skin was stung by sharp grains of flying sand. The wind had suddenly whipped up a fierce sandstorm.

Annie could not see much – just a few shadowy figures. But she heard something that sent an icy shiver down her spine. Right next to her, a man and a woman were speaking in hoarse whispers. As she heard the man speak, she knew she was listening to the voice of whoever had stolen the idol. Both voices were familiar. They were passengers on the boat, but she didn't know exactly who they belonged to.

The thief said no more. Instead she heard the others, all talking at once. The Professor was urging everyone not to panic and Drusilla was wailing as usual. In addition, Annie definitely identified the voices of two other passengers. That left just four passengers as possible suspects.

DON'T TURN THE PAGE YET

Whose voices did Annie identify? Who are the possible suspects?

20

H-h-he-help.
I d-d-don't like
s-s-sandstorms.

The curse! The curse!
The ancient gods have
sent this storm to curse
us all.

Most unusual and very
peculiar. Perhaps it's
the curse at work.

Be quiet. Stop
wittering. Ouch!
This sand hurts.

Ma che scemo!
Mama mia!

It's all right . . . Don't
panic . . . It's just a
sandstorm . . . Keep
calm . . . Follow me.

21

Interrogation

Annie followed the Professor's voice back to the boat. She half expected to find one of the passengers missing but they were all there and not one of them looked guilty. So the thief had not made a getaway. Why not?

Ahmed Ablunda, the local Police Chief, arrived and put everyone under boat arrest. Annie found it all quite exciting – she had never been a suspect before.

Annie couldn't wait to be interrogated. She was itching to tell the police chief what she had heard. But when her turn came, he did not seem at all interested.

Instead, he asked her silly, meaningless questions. . . . Where is the Baron? What is the number of the Swiss bank account? Where is the golden mask, the doubloons and the pieces of eight?

WITNESSES' STATEMENTS

H. EILSN — It was dark for 60 seconds

T. TURPPIS — the light went out for about one minute

D. DE VISP — I heard a banging noise

S. SCOOP — I heard nothing

Prof. P. POH — I went to the ladder — no one left on entering the chamber

D. P. GLYNN — the floor of the chamber was damp like a beach

Dr BOTTLN — the maps were more complete half and floor

Annie decided he was a useless detective and probably half mad. She was closer to solving the mystery than he was, so she would do some snooping on her own. But did he have any information that would help her?

Then she spotted a piece of yellow paper destined for the rubbish bin. It was covered in the Police Chief's strange scrawl. Was it Arabic? No!

She waited for a moment when he wasn't looking, picked something out of her bag and used it to decipher the scrawl. She was not sure if it was useful or not. Still, it might come in handy later.

DON'T TURN THE PAGE YET

What did Annie take out of her bag?
What is written on the yellow paper?

Footprints in the Sand

Back in her cabin, Annie tried to piece together the clues she had gathered. But they didn't make sense at all and thinking about them gave her brain ache. Then a brilliant thought struck her. The photos! Perhaps they would help.

Annie picked out one of the photos taken just after the idol vanished. Around the empty stone block were four sets of fresh footprints.

Annie's brain started to work at double speed . . . Whoever took the idol must have been near the block – close enough to lift the idol off it. So one set of footprints must belong to the thief.

Annie was very impressed by her brilliant bit of brain work. But how could she discover whose footprints they were? She worked out an ingenious plan.

After supper, Annie left the other passengers playing Egyptian snakes and ladders and crept along the corridor towards the cabins. Just as she expected, they had all left their day shoes outside their doors to be cleaned. Swiftly and silently, she crept between the cabins, checking each pair of shoes against the photo she clutched in her hand.

At the end of her search, she knew that at last she was close to finding the thief.

DON'T TURN THE PAGE YET

Whose shoes made the prints?

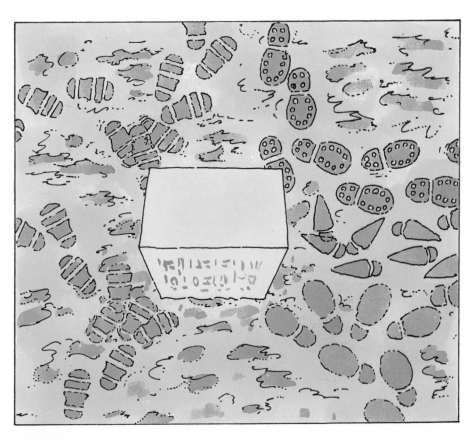

PROFESSOR POTT'S
DESERT BOOTS

TERRY TRUBBLE'S TRAINERS

DEVILLA'S STILETTOS

DRUSILLA'S
FLIP-FLOPS

SAM SCOOP'S SNEAKERS

ANNIE'S BASEBALL BOOTS

LUIGI MACARONI'S
WINKLE PICKERS

HARRIET'S SPIKEY BOOTS

DR BOFFIN'S BROGUES

Photo Clues

Annie sneaked back to her cabin feeling very pleased with herself. She had narrowed down the list of suspects. Now another mystery began to bug her. She wanted to know what had become of the idol. Where was it?

The idol was much too big and bulky to slip into a pocket. In fact it would be impossible to remove it from the chamber hidden anywhere – in a bag, under a jacket, inside a shirt – without it showing. Unless . . .

Two photos caught her eye. They were both taken in the panic after the idol had vanished. Annie stared hard at them. Something puzzled her. Something about the chamber was wrong, or different from the way she remembered it.

In a flash Annie knew exactly where the idol was. She must go and investigate IMMEDIATELY!

DON'T TURN THE PAGE YET

Where is the idol?

Back to the Chamber

But Annie couldn't leave straight away. The other passengers started playing moonlit deck quoits right outside her cabin. So she waited until everyone had gone to bed.

She crept out on to the deck trying hard to avoid Ahmed Ablunda's men. To her dismay, the gangplank was guarded. A dozy policeman slouched against the railing, but his dog was wide awake and growling.

Annie had a brainwave. She hopped over the railing with her bag of junk and slid down a mooring rope to the shore.

Once she was on dry land, Annie looked at the moonlit landscape. Which way was the buried chamber?

Annie had a second brainwave. She rummaged in her bag for the map the man with the moustache had given her. The buried chamber was not marked and she did not know where the boat was moored. Then she remembered her journey earlier that day. Now she knew how to get there.

DON'T TURN THE PAGE YET

Where is the chamber and what is Annie's route?

REFRESHMENT STANDS

RUINS OF PHARAOH'S PALACE

RIVERSIDE VILLAGE

TWO PYRAMIDS

SMALL SPHINX

RUINED PALACE

OASIS

HILLS

MORE TOMBS

PHARAOHS' TOMBS

ANCIENT SHRINE

THE GREAT DESERT PYRAMID

OBELISK

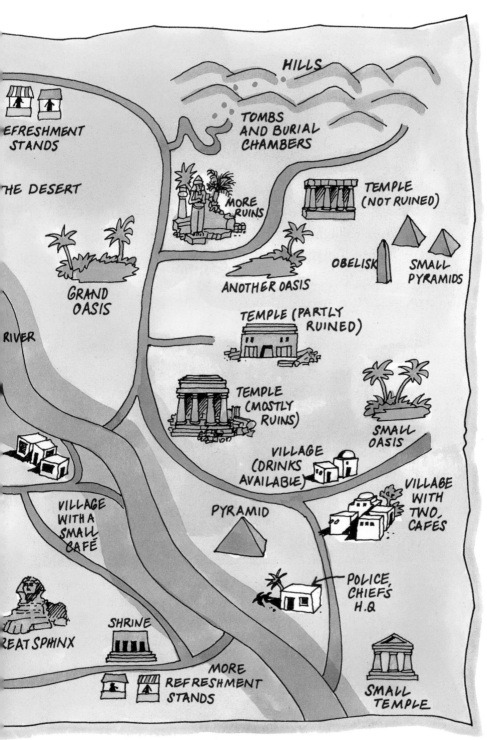

REFRESHMENT STANDS

THE DESERT

GRAND OASIS

RIVER

HILLS

TOMBS AND BURIAL CHAMBERS

MORE RUINS

TEMPLE (NOT RUINED)

ANOTHER OASIS

OBELISK

SMALL PYRAMIDS

TEMPLE (PARTLY RUINED)

TEMPLE (MOSTLY RUINS)

SMALL OASIS

VILLAGE (DRINKS AVAILABLE)

VILLAGE WITH TWO CAFES

VILLAGE WITH A SMALL CAFÉ

PYRAMID

POLICE CHIEF'S H.Q

GREAT SPHINX

SHRINE

MORE REFRESHMENT STANDS

SMALL TEMPLE

The Crooks Return

Inside the buried chamber, Annie found the idol exactly where she thought it would be. All of a sudden, she heard a noise at the top of the shaft. Horrified, she recognized the voice of the thief speaking to his accomplice. Annie had to think fast. She must protect the idol at all costs!

She grabbed it and shoved it into her big bag – she was surprised how light it felt. Then she pressed herself against the wall hoping to hide in the gloom. She kept perfectly still. She heard two voices talking in hoarse whispers and she could just make out two shadows creeping across the chamber. Then she heard someone scrabbling frantically in the sand. They were looking for the idol! She knew she had to make a dash for it before the crooks discovered the idol was missing.

Too late! As Annie clambered up the first few rungs of the ladder, she felt a strong hand grasp her leg. She tried to grab it and push it away but she got a head instead – she felt hair, an ear and something sharp that scratched her hand. Then suddenly she was free. The thief must have lost his balance.

There was no time to lose. She had to stop the thief escaping, but he was already starting to climb the ladder. Could she trap him in the chamber? The knots securing the ladder were too tight to undo and she couldn't budge the boulder. She could cut the ropes but there was nothing sharp lying around that she could see. In the nick of time, Annie knew she was being thick. Of course she could trap him.

DON'T TURN THE PAGE YET

How does Annie trap the thief?

The Mystery Thickens

As Annie made her way back to the boat, she began to feel frightened. She tried to pull herself together – but she knew she wasn't just being silly. It really was very scary scrambling across a strange desert all alone in the middle of the night carrying a priceless idol.

And what about the curse? Annie hoped that the powers of the ancient gods would not mistake her for the thief and punish her. She started to run.

By the time she reached the gangplank, she was too exhausted to worry about the guards. She only remembered them when she passed the policeman and his dog, both fast asleep.

She made straight for her cabin and bolted the door. She knew she ought to take the idol straight to the Police Chief, but first she wanted to look at it herself. As she lifted it from her bag, something in the back of her mind worried her. What was it?

She turned it round slowly, looking at it from every angle – front, back and from both sides. The more she stared at it, the more it bothered her. In a flash she realized what was wrong. It could only mean one thing . . .

She had to act fast. Should she go to the Police Chief? No, not yet. He may not accept her story and he would waste valuable time.

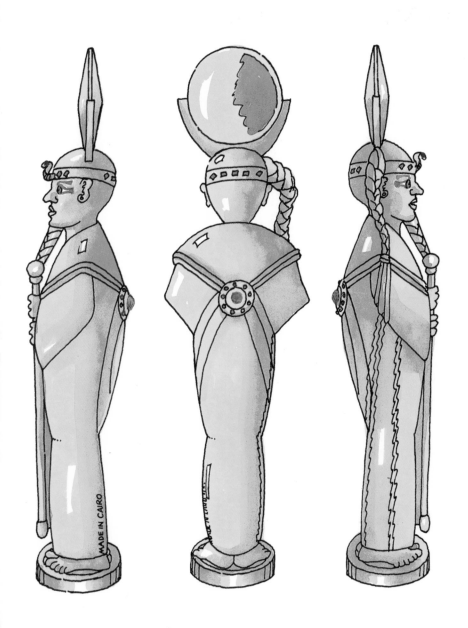

Annie racked her brains. Who could she trust? The Professor! He was sure to believe her story. She set off for his cabin.

DON'T TURN THE PAGE YET

**What is wrong with the idol?
What does this mean?**

In the Professor's Cabin

The Professor's door was unlocked. She nervously poked her head round the door frame and peeped inside, expecting to see the Professor fast asleep. But he was nowhere to be seen.

His cabin was not exactly empty. It was crammed from floor to ceiling with the most incredible collection of junk. There was nowhere to sit – not even on the floor, so she just stood gaping at the Professor's peculiar possessions.

Then she saw something that made her go weak at the knees. Could it be? At first she refused to believe her eyes. She looked again and this time she was certain she was staring straight at it.

Annie didn't know what to think. She slumped on to the Professor's bunk, on top of all the rubbish, feeling very, very miserable. This spoilt everything. All her cunning detective work and all her brilliant theories were wrong . . . or were they?

DON'T TURN THE PAGE YET

What did Annie spot amongst the Professor's belongings?

35

The Professor's Story

Just then, the Professor bounced into the room followed by the little person with the moustache. Annie jumped up, suddenly feeling very brave.

"YOU stole it," she shouted at the Professor, in her fiercest voice.

For a moment, the Professor looked puzzled. Then, instead of looking guilty or frightened, he smiled and began to explain.

"No, I didn't steal it, I'm looking after it. You must believe me. I knew the idol was in danger and so I had a copy made. I am bound by the curse to protect the idol. Who knows what might have happened otherwise."

Annie was confused. Was he telling the truth? She felt certain that he was, so she told him the whole story.

"I told you she was clever," the little person squeaked

"Well done," said the Professor slapping Annie heartily on the back. "The Police Chief has drawn a complete blank but you've already trapped the Doppel Gang!"

"The what?" spluttered Annie.

SILAS 'SPIKEY' SCARFACE

Known to be an expert thief but no criminal record so far. Left leg is shorter than right leg.

JOHN SMITH (alias Angus McHaggis, Michel Paté and Hans Sauerkraut.) A genius at foreign languages and accents. This man is ruthless.

The Professor produced an impressive looking police file and pulled out six official documents.

"The Doppel Gang," said the Professor pointing at the documents. "These are the crooks

36

EUSTACE WHIMPE

Very short and skinny. Has a constantly bad cough and a weedy voice. Whines a lot.

GLORIA GOLDFINGER

Tall, slim and vain. Hair colour changes often. Fond of expensive jewellery. Thought to be the brains of the gang.

DORIS DANE-JURASS

A schoolgirl - the youngest member of the gang. Crafty and cunning but looks innocent. Sometimes wears a wig.

BARON GRABBITT

Gang leader. A power crazy, highly dangerous millionaire. His home, Grabbitt Castle, is probably the gang's H.Q.

who are after the idol."

Annie stared at the documents. Her heart sank. She recognized two of the crooks as passengers on the boat. But were they the thieves?

DON'T TURN THE PAGE YET

Which members of the Doppel Gang are disguised as passengers on the boat?

The Truth at Last!

Having picked out the Doppel Gang members, Annie and the Professor went to the Police Chief. This time he DID believe her – the Professor made sure of it .

Then things started happening very quickly. Almost before she knew it, Annie was setting off once more for the buried chamber. This time she was on official police business which meant she travelled by camel.

Annie found camel riding rather tricky. She was trying hard to balance when she noticed her hand – the one she had scratched in her struggle with the thief. It was marked with blue pen.

At the same time, the uncomfortable rolling movement of the camel jolted her brain into action. At last, all the clues slotted into place. She knew for sure that she had been right all along.

Then Annie caught sight of two figures at the entrance to the chamber.

"The crooks! They've escaped," shrieked the police chief. "Stop them at once!"

There was a lot of noise as the police struggled with the crooks. Only when they were handcuffed was Annie's voice heard.

"They're not the ones. The thief and his accomplice are still in the chamber. I know who did it and I know why."

DON'T TURN THE PAGE YET

Is Annie right?
    Who is the thief and why did he do it?
    Who is his accomplice?

Afterwards

Reluctantly, the Police Chief listened to Annie's protests. He dismounted his camel rather clumsily and shuffled towards the hole in the ground. From the bottom of the shaft came the noise of desperate, muffled whispers.

By this time it was completely light and the wind was starting to blow. In the distance, Annie saw an ominous sandy cloud. Another sandstorm?

All of a sudden a vicious gust of wind blew Annie to the ground. As she struggled to her feet, she screamed in horror.

"LOOK OUT!" she yelled to the Police Chief.

The big boulder that Annie had been unable to budge was rolling towards the Police Chief. He threw himself clear only just in time. A split second later it would have squashed him flat.

Annie watched in disbelief. The boulder had stopped, lodged in the hole leading down to the chamber. The entrance to the chamber was sealed and the crooks were trapped inside.

"But that boulder weighs tons," Annie thought aloud. "It's impossible. How did it happen? Was it the wind . . .?"

"Or the CURSE," said the Professor seriously. "The ancient gods have taken their revenge."

Everyone turned and stared at the Professor in stunned silence. Was it true? Was it really the ancient curse punishing the thief? Annie did not want to believe it, but there seemed to be no other explanation.

Afterwards, when Annie's adventure in Egypt was over, there was still one other thing that puzzled her. Who was the little person with the outsize moustache?

Do you know?

Clues

Page 6

Match the symbols in the Professor's notebook with those on the stone block. You will need to add a few small words (such as a, the, of and who) for the curse to make sense in English.

Page 8

Test each god's answer in turn and see if it is possible for that one to be telling the truth while the other two are lying.

Hint: When one god who is lying accuses another, second, god of lying, it means this second god must be telling the truth.

Page 10

The port side is the left side of a boat and the stern is the back. The front of a boat is more pointed than the back. A boat with a stern deck may have other decks as well.

Page 12

Try following the instructions from each starting point. You do not need to go in the direction of the arrows.

Page 14

The clues lie in the scribbled notes. Have a good look at what people are saying and the clothes they are wearing.

Page 16

This is easy but the spelling is awful.

Page 20

There are two clues in the text. The scribbled notes on the passenger list might help (see page 14).

Page 22

The Police Chief writes from right to left. Look on page 10 to find out what Annie keeps in her bag.

Page 24

Look very carefully at the soles of the shoes. Take special notice of studs, grooves and ridges. Think what sort of print they would make.

Page 26

No one is holding or concealing the idol. Could it be hidden somewhere else? Pages 18-19 and 22-23 may give you some clues.

Page 28

Look on page 18 for the landmarks Annie passed. The pictures on page 4 may help you to pinpoint the entrance to the chamber.

Page 30

Think of the things Annie keeps in her bag (see page 10).

Page 32

Compare the idol with its description in The Daily Wheeze on page 9. Sapphires are blue and emeralds are green.

Page 34

This is easy. Use your eyes.

Page 36

Look at features which are hard to alter or hide such as noses, ears and scars.

Page 38

Who carries a blue pen? Look on pages 30-31 for more clues.

Page 40

His disguise isn't very good. His hair, glasses and squeaky voice give him away.

Answers

Here you can see what the curse means in English.

Here stands (the) idol (of the) moon god. Many evil men

want (to) steal (the) idol. (The) first man (who) sees (the) idol

must protect (the) idol from evil men. (A) curse strikes all

thieves and any man (who) disobeys these words.

Pages 8-9

Horus stole the golden apple. Horus and Anubis were lying. Osiris was telling the truth.

Pages 10-11

The SS CHAOS is the only boat that fits the description.

Annie goes to the Long Room. The black line shows the route she takes.

Annie starts here.

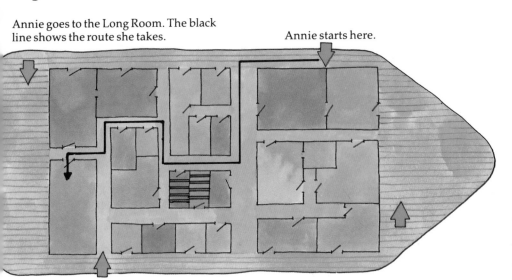

Here are the names of the passengers on the boat.

Professor Pott

Dr Boffin

Drusilla P. Culia

Terry Trubble

The waiters are the ones wearing hats like this.

Harriet Flash

This person's name is missing.

Devilla de Visp

Luigi Macaroni

Sam Scoop

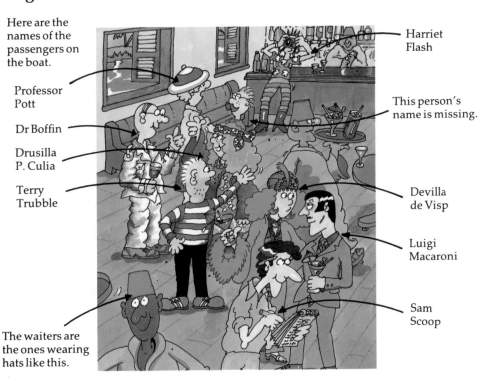

Pages 16-17

With the spelling corrected, the message says:

THE IDOL IS IN GREAT DANGER. A BUNCH OF RUTHLESS CROOKS ARE AFTER IT AND I AM WORRIED. REMEMBER THE CURSE OF THE IDOL ... IT WILL TAKE ITS REVENGE. KEEP YOUR EYES OPEN AND BEWARE. TRUST NO ONE. GOOD LUCK.

P.S. HERE IS A MAP. IT MIGHT BE USEFUL. YOU NEVER KNOW.

Pages 20-21

Annie recognizes the voices of Professor Pott, Drusilla P. Culia, Luigi Macaroni and Terry Trubble. These four can be ruled out as suspects. This leaves Dr Boffin, Sam Scoop, Devilla de Visp and Harriet Flash as possible suspects.

It's all right . . . Don't panic! . . . It's just a sandstorm . . . Keep calm . . . Follow me.

The Professor – Annie recognized his voice urging everyone not to panic.

Ma che scemo! Mama mia!

Luigi Macaroni – his Italian gives him away.

The curse! The curse! The ancient gods have sent this storm to curse us all.

Drusilla. – Annie heard her wailing as usual, just as she did in the chamber.

H-h-he-help. I d-d-don't like s-s-sandstorms.

Terry Trubble – he has a terrible stutter.

Pages 22-23

The Police Chief's notes are written back to front and the piece of paper is upside down. Annie takes her pocket mirror from her bag to read the notes (see page 10). She turns the paper the other way up and holds it in front of the mirror. Do the same thing and you can find out what is written on the yellow paper.

Pages 24-25

The footprints in the sand were made by Professor Pott, Luigi Macaroni, Sam Scoop and Dr Boffin. This means that one of these four is the thief.

Professor Pott's boot prints

Luigi Macaroni's winkle-picker prints

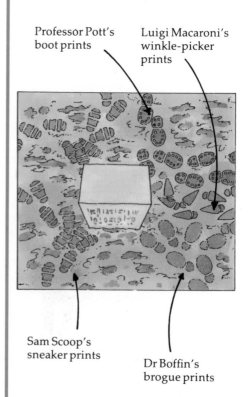

Sam Scoop's sneaker prints

Dr Boffin's brogue prints

Pages 26-27

The idol is still in the chamber. No one could have taken the idol out of the chamber as the photographs show that no one is holding or concealing it. In the suspicious conversation on page 20, the thief reveals that he does not have the idol on him.

The idol is buried in the sandy floor. Annie heard the thief doing this when the lights went out (see page 19). So did Devilla de Visp (see page 23).

The idol is buried under this mound.

Pages 28-29

The black line shows Annie's route from the river to the chamber. The entrance is in a direct line with two pyramids and an obelisk (see page 4).

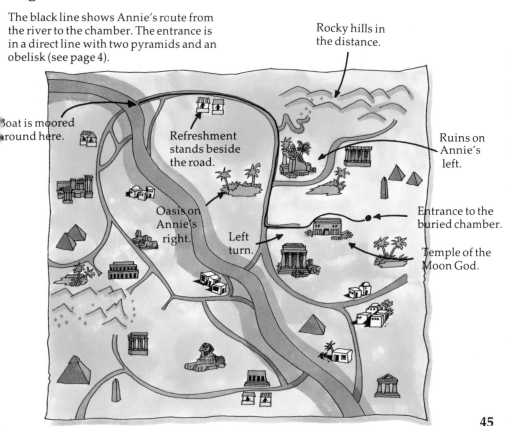

Rocky hills in the distance.

Boat is moored around here.

Refreshment stands beside the road.

Oasis on Annie's right.

Left turn.

Ruins on Annie's left.

Entrance to the buried chamber.

Temple of the Moon God.

Pages 30-31

Annie cuts the ropes at the top of the ladder with her extra strong penknife. She always carries this in her bag (see page 10).

The thief climbing up falls back down the shaft with the ladder and is trapped in the chamber.

Pages 32-33

There are four differences between the idol and the description in The Daily Wheeze (see page 9). It is also much lighter than the real idol. Professor Pott

and Eric notice how heavy it is but Annie is surprised by how light it is. The modern factory stamp shows it must be a fake.

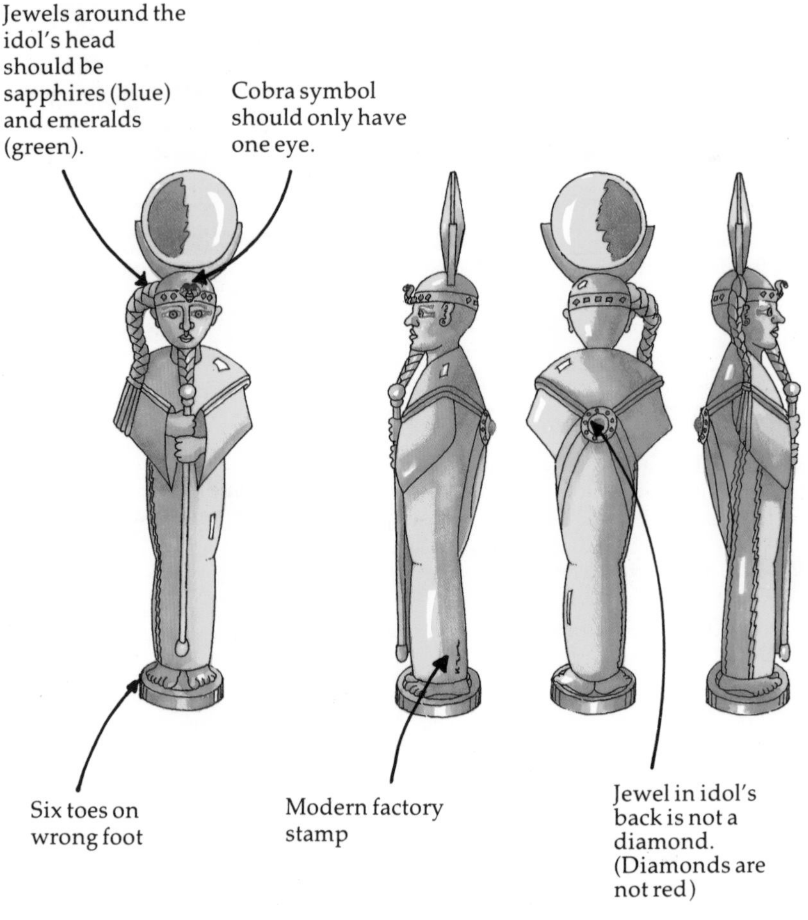

Jewels around the idol's head should be sapphires (blue) and emeralds (green).

Cobra symbol should only have one eye.

Six toes on wrong foot

Modern factory stamp

Jewel in idol's back is not a diamond. (Diamonds are not red)

Annie spots the idol half hidden beneath the lampshade on the chest of drawers. It is recognizable by the six toes on its left foot and the moon disk on its head which is just visible at the top of the shade.

Pages 36-37

The two crooks are John Smith, disguised as Luigi Macaroni and Gloria Goldfinger, disguised as Devilla de Visp.

Ahmed Ablunda must have thought that Annie was Doris Dane-Jurass in disguise (see page 22). In fact they are quite different.

He has dyed his brown hair black.

Scar on left cheek.

Button nose.

Shape of nose is distinctive and hard to disguise.

No moustache usually. He has grown one as a disguise.

Same gold earrings and necklace.

She has changed her hair colour, but it is the same style and length.

The thief is Sam Scoop. A series of clues leads Annie to discover this.

In the sandstorm (see page 20), Annie does not recognise his voice. This means he could have held the suspicious conversation and makes him a suspect alongside Dr Boffin, Devilla de Visp and Harriet Flash. Annie rules out the two women because she knows the thief is a man. Annie identifies four sets of footprints (see page 24). She dismisses Professor Pott and Luigi Macaroni as suspects because she recognized their voices in the sandstorm. This leaves just two suspects: Dr Boffin and Sam Scoop.

When Annie returns to the chamber (see page 30), she hears the thief telling his accomplice that he stole the idol because it would make a good story. Annie remembers the cryptic comment beside Sam Scoop's name on the passenger list (see page 14). Now she definitely suspects Sam Scoop and not Dr Boffin.

When she discovers the real idol in the Professor's cabin and identifies the members of the Doppel Gang, Annie's theories are thrown into confusion. But not for long. While riding the camel, she notices the blue mark (see page 38). She remembers her struggle with the thief. She grabbed his head and scratched her hand on something sharp. Sam Scoop always carries a blue pen behind his ear.

Harriet Flash is Sam Scoop's accomplice. Annie knows the accomplice is a woman. She rules out Drusilla immediately because she recognizes her voice in the sandstorm (see page 20). This leaves Devilla and Harriet. When Sam Scoop returns to the chamber (see page 30), he calls his accomplice "Harry". In the gloom, Harriet's boot is just visible. These clues, plus the fact that Harriet is a good friend of Sam Scoop (see page 14), make Annie suspect Harriet. She cannot be certain until she sees Devilla, the other suspect, captured by the police at the chamber entrance (see page 38).

It's Eric. He disguised himself and was not named on the passenger list to assist the Professor and to do some snooping in case of a theft. Eric knew Annie since they are in the same class at school. He also knew that Annie was a brilliant puzzle solver and reckoned she would be very useful if the idol really was in danger. In fact, Annie solved the mystery long before Eric even came close.

This edition first published in 2002 by Usborne Publishing Ltd., Usborne House, 83-85 Saffron Hill, London EC1N 8RT, England. www.usborne.com Copyright © 2002, 1986 Usborne Publishing Ltd. The name Usborne and the devices ♀♔ are Trade Marks of Usborne Publishing Ltd. Printed in China.